A Prelude to Dancing with Giants

Christopher Croucher,
Stormdancer

Faery Cat Press

A Prelude to Dancing with Giants is a small book but not a small feat. Things like this don't happen on their own or in a vacuum, especially for a first-timer like me. With that in mind, I would like to thank everyone who made it possible for me to do this kind of magic...

Burdock, thank you first for saying "yes you can" and offering to publish this work. Without that, this book simply would not be here.

Thank you Holly, for your writer's wisdom and kind but clear guidance for my composition. Your notes helped me bring my stories to life.

Thank you Marc and Molly, Jonathan, Ali, Claire, Thomas, Hayleigh, and all the wonderful friends who lent a listening ear or a reader's eye, as well as thoughts and suggestions along the way, helping me to clear up the many dancing thoughts in my head.

Thank you to my dear friends and mentors in the EarthSpirit Community, without whom, my magic(k) would not be what it is today. Thank you Moira, Irene, Juniper, Trey and Wolfhame, Rose and Jac, and of course Deirdre, and many others, for helping me to cultivate my magic(k)al work in ways I could not have imagined.

Thank you Meg, for helping me to see that, while I stir many cauldrons, they're all important. Though they may take a while to come to fruition, when they do, they'll be stronger for the time they took.

And to Koti, who sat on my feet, thank you for keeping them warm while I finished writing.

And beyond all of the specific ways you've all helped me along the path, I am deeply grateful for your support in all the day-to-day ways you are there for me.

But there are two people who deserve acknowledgement and gratitude far more than I could ever give...First, my father, Richard, whose love of writing and art passed to me. Every now and then, I notice how similar we are, and that makes me smile. I miss you deeply as I carry on what you taught me.

And finally, my mother, Judy, who is everything in this world to me. Without you, I would not be able to do any of what I do. Your creativity flows through me, but it is your generosity and support of all of my fantastical endeavors that have made it possible for any of this work to exist. I love you.

Thank you all.

INTRODUCTION

Welcome to *A Prelude to Dancing with Giants*. This book, a collection of essays and stories, musings and how-tos, a little bit of poetry and some pieces of art, is a new step in a dance that I have been doing, and perhaps didn't know I was doing, for quite some time now.

When I was in college, I made a dance piece that included a solo for myself that took place, in silence, between two group sections. Dressed all in dark blue, the first moves I made were in the upstage corner, shadowed and internal, hidden in dramatically dim light. Then something shifted. I stood up on pointe and I walked in a strong, straight line on my toes, from the back of the stage to the front, the lights brightening as I strode forward, my gaze proud ahead of me. This book is that walk forward.

For over twenty-five years, I've been exploring, studying, and practicing magic(k)*. This experience, spanning more than three quarters of my life, has been filled with excitement, trepidation, elation, frustration, great happiness, and deep sadness, but more than anything else, love and joy. Through my love of Magic, I have found inspiration, comfort, and fulfillment. I have found Connection with Nature, Community, and Spirit, capitalized here because they form such potent parts of my life. I have found purpose and meaning, but until recently, much of my dance with magic(k) has been in the comfortable shade of my own dramatic lighting.

For a little over a decade though, I've been taking steps forward, teaching and sharing my experience and love of magic(k). For a little over half that time, I've been settling into my Work, capitalized, here again, because it is far more than a job; it is my Calling. I have shared my interest in spell work and foundations of magickal practice. I have taught meditation and aspects of psychic techniques. I have practiced and taught forms of divination. Most recently, however, I have found the balance point, the crossroads where my spiritual practice meets my practical training. It is the place where magic(k), movement, and nature come together. The introduction to that balance point, the point from which I can walk forward strongly into the bright lights, to share the thing that I really love, is what you'll find in this book.

In every bio that I write, including the one you'll find herein, I begin with some version of *Christopher Croucher, Stormdancer, is an artist, performer, healer, and witch.* This is a very succinct way of touching on the facets of my work all at once. I am an artist in many forms, a dancer and performer, a massage therapist and magickal healer, and of course, a witch. This book is an introduction to those facets and each section shines a light on an aspect of the work. I am sharing it with you for the simple reason that I love what I do and I am working towards doing more of it. I am enthralled when I can offer up my love of the practice and see the light in someone's eyes when they really feel Magic for the first time or get to sink deeper into their experience of it. That is why this book is in your hands.

So here it is, *A Prelude to Dancing with Giants*.

*We'll get to the *why* of the parenthesis soon.

Section I: Movement and Magic(k)

MOVEMENT AND
MAGIC(K)

The first section of this book is about Movement and Magick. At the root of the vast majority of my work, you'll find my lifelong love of dance and my equally long-lived love of magic(k). The two are foundational for me.

That being said, I know that *dance* can be a daunting word for many people. It calls up feelings of nervousness and inadequacy, born of botched dance recitals and awkward boogying on the dance floor at a distant cousin's wedding. *Magic(k)* can be an equally complicated word. It has connotations that reach into cultural assumptions and experiences of being called crazy, childish, and even evil.

In this first section, I want to lay a little bit of groundwork and offer a bit of a warm-up into my viewpoint on Movement and Magick. It is not an exhaustive study by any means, but I hope that it might begin to set aside any stubborn doubts on the subject and bring some clarity to definitions and practices as they pertain to this work. More than that, I hope it raises some interest, ideas, and even inspiration as you consider what Movement and Magick might be for you.

Let the dance begin!

Movement, Dance, the Dancer, and Magic(k)

"Movements are as eloquent as words." - Isadora Duncan

Movement

I am, both by training and by nature, a dancer. I used to put on shows for my parents in our living room, dancing little choreographed pieces before I ever knew what a dance class was. But being drawn to dancing like that is most certainly not the case for everyone.

HOWEVER

And that's a big however, movement is, quite literally, for everyone. Over the years of my art and dance practice, I have come to think of movement in the broadest and most inclusive sense of the term. If we are breathing, we are moving. If our hearts are beating, we are moving. To take it to its farthest point, even as our bodies return to the earth in death we are moving, the particles that make up our being returning to the greater movement of Everything.

So, movement is everything and everything is movement, even in moments of stillness. The wonderful thing about this understanding of movement is that it necessarily means that anyone, of any level of training or physical ability, can engage in movement. It is mutable and malleable, scalable, and is accessible for anyone who is called to develop the use of movement as a skill.

The concept of movement, as I am describing it for use in magick, is infinitely broad. Being that everything is movement, a simple gesture, done with intention, can be a spell or ritual. Movements used for magick may be singular or repeated, basic or complex, traditional or extemporized. They may be as uncomplicated as walking or as intricate as tying complicated knots in a cord. They may be a wave of the hand or a symbolic action, the drawing of runes in the air with the arms or scoring spirals into the soil with the feet. They may include a tool such as a wand or broom, and the intrinsic movements that accompany them, casting or sweeping a Circle for instance. Even intentional breath, the rest of the body otherwise still, is magickal movement. It is quite common for movement to be taken for granted or glossed over, largely because movement is our natural state of being, but if we bring attention to the movements inherent in our practices and the meaning within them, they take on an added power of their own.

The method of moving also offers infinite possibility. Movements such as writing or typing, knitting or weaving, biking or driving, yoga or tai chi, shopping or writing a check, anything at all that requires movement, which is quite literally anything, can be woven into a magickal act. Two of my personal favorites are spinning yarn, which immediately shifts me into a meditative state because of the repetitive and rhythmic movements paired with the transformational act of creativity, and running or walking on a treadmill, which has become one of my favorite ways to do magickal work because the physical exertion leads to a trance-like state perfect for journeying and meditation. Moreover, each type of movement can carry inherent meaning. The physical exertion of exercise may denote a willingness to work towards a goal. The use of crafting or creating artwork may be symbolic of tapping into the imagination to create new realities. The movements used to pay for an item might be used in rituals for prosperity. To drive the point home, like hammering a nail, which is also a perfectly useful and meaningful motion, the possibilities of movement are endless.

When applying these movements to ritual and magick, they can play any number of roles. Depending on the tradition, culture, purpose, and style of practice, the use of movement can vary greatly. Movements can delineate a boundary or container of sacred space. They can be used in prayer or to convey the symbolic meaning of a ritual. They can bring about an altered state of consciousness or trance state. At its core, though, in its most basic of functions, movement is, by its very nature, energy. In each and every movement that occurs, there is a measure of potential energy that transforms into kinetic energy. This scientific reality translates into the spiritual concept that movement is one of the easiest ways to raise energy for magick and ritual, and in that spiritual context, movement also gives meaning to that energy.

Dance

And then there's dance. When I was studying dance in my undergraduate years at Bard College, I was confronted with the very post-modern idea that "everything is dance." I really struggled with that notion and there are many professional dancers who might also. Dance, to me, was a choreographed set of movements that matched up with a song. Over time, and with no small amount of resistance, I began to understand what the concept of everything being dance really meant. It's not necessarily true that everything is, in actuality, dance, but rather that it is possible to bring any movement into the realm of dance. Beyond the technical pliés, tendus, jumps, turns, kicks, and splits that ride the beat of a pre-recorded song, exploring movement for its own sake, with or without a soundtrack, is an act of dance. Sipping a cup, turning a door handle, kicking a ball, petting a cat, are all movements that can be brought into dance. That is a very powerful notion for our magickal work because it means that we have endless ways to use dance to enact magick.

Consider a spell for healing, let's say, a broken leg. One might choreograph a ritual dance that tells the story of the leg being broken, the subject being laid up, the magick working on the leg, and then the subject walking again with ease. That is just one tiny example in a sea of possibilities.

So, if everything can be dance and movement is intrinsically in everything, what is the difference? For the purposes of the magickal work that I am proposing here, I describe dance as something that is structured and intentional, even in the loosest of ways. Dance is self-contained, bringing movements together and differentiating them from the commonplace actions intrinsic in the everyday or the movements of non-dance-specific rituals. It takes movement to the next level of intentionality, giving it duration, repetition, and a more complex purpose than movement on its own. It creates patterns of form and flow. It sometimes tells a story and generally has an arc of some kind, a beginning and an end, whether or not it is detailing a specific narrative.

Dance may factor into magick in a wide range of ways. A set dance piece or an opportunity for ecstatic, non-choreographed dance may be built into a ritual, sometimes as a container, sometimes as a focal point. A dance performance may be a ritual or magickal working in and of itself, done for an audience. A larger ritual may be the container for a dance experience, such as a traditional circle dance or a drum-and-dance for trance work. Some rituals may be formed entirely of a dance, choreographed or designed with all the components of ritual included within it.

Admittedly, it feels as if I'm opening this discussion by saying that everything is possible and we can engage however we want, which leaves us with very few boundaries and borders to work within. In many ways, that is true. With all the possible intersectionalities of spiritual practice and personal experience, training in magick or movement, cultural nuances, and personal preferences, what I am suggesting is just the very broad beginning of a much wider discussion of how movement and dance meld with magickal work. Movement is everything, everything can be dance, dance can be used in nearly any way in ritual and magick...With all of these possibilities in mind, I would say, again for our purposes here, that movement and dance are similar in many ways while also being on a spectrum or continuum. Pick any point on that continuum between movement and dance and you will find a powerful and effective way of creating and engaging in magick.

The Dancer

Many people I have worked with, both in ritual dance and performance settings, have adamantly claimed that they are not dancers. One circus performer that I worked with for a dance performance rebuffed me every time I called them a dancer, saying that they didn't have the training to be a dancer.

They were very clearly uncomfortable claiming the term, even though we were choreographing and dancing together and performing in a post-modern dance style. In that case, I had to call them a "mover" to satisfy their own inner expectation and self-identification. This person looked at me, with a background in ballet and modern dance, as a true "dancer," and sometimes that is all anyone can see.

What, then, makes someone a "dancer"? As I've said, some might argue that training or technical skill defines the dancer. I am not going to make that argument. Now, it may be true that an audience might not want to pay to see a stage production in which the dancers have no training, largely because the lack of technical skill would, by necessity, take away from the experience of the audience and likely the intention of the work as a whole. That is, however, an isolated situation. Though a person who dances without training may not be a professional, it is not the title of professional that determines who is and who is not a dancer.

Instead, I like to think that someone is defined by their verbs. I make art and so I am an artist. Someone writes and so they are a writer. Someone else sings and so they are a singer. Again, this is not to say that they are "professionals" or that they need to define themselves this way to be effective at what they do. The fact that they do a particular thing defines them as someone who does that thing. It's a straightforward and simplistic way to look at it, but I think that is best in this case. It passes beyond the walls of gatekeeping and includes anyone who is called to do something about which they are passionate. Imposter syndrome be damned!

Therefore, someone who dances is a dancer.

And Magic(k)

And finally, there's Magic(k). There are many historical and personal ways to describe magic. One of the most common is Aleister Crowley's, "the Science and Art of causing Change to occur in conformity with Will." I have a bit more of a nuanced definition, largely because I like to think of *magic* and *magick* as two parts of a whole. On the grander scale, I tend to describe "magic" as an intangible and powerful sense of Connection to the Self and the World and the effects that tapping into that Connection can have. I leave it broad because it can include all sorts of experiences, from enjoying a particularly moving painting or seeing the first sliver of a crescent moon in the glow of the setting sun, to feeling the fully-embodied connective power of a ritual.

"Magick," to me, describes a more technical application. I define "magick" as the ways, devices, and techniques we use to reach the magical feeling of Connection. Spells, rituals, incantations, potions, divination, and any other means of connecting to magic, are all magick. The spelling shift, adding the 'k' at the end, comes from a long line of traditions that use altered spelling of the word to differentiate between stage magic and the magic of fantasy from the practice of spiritual and practical magick. In my personal work and writing, and totally by personal preference, when I spell it with parenthesis, "magic(k)," I am referring to both the technical practice and the spirit behind it at the same time.

And so, taking all of these nuanced definitions together, we arrive at the nexus of the Magickal Dancer, one who intentionally uses movement and dance as the tools and means to enact magick and bring about magic. As is the case in the world of choreography, dance, and indeed art in general, as well as spirituality broadly, there are no hard and fast rules. There are ways to train; there are ways to simply jump in and experience. There are ways to create within a structure; there are ways to improvise.

There are ways to cast spells; there are ways to simply revel in the energy. The practice of being a Magickal Dancer is infinitely mutable and, like most things, is only limited, defined, and supported by what is brought in by the practitioner. Like all tools and practices for the purpose, it is a doorway into Magic.

DANCE: A GIFT FROM AND FOR THE GODS

There are a scarce few species that possess the particular cognitive faculties that allow them to dance. By scientific definition, the requirements for the biological capacity to dance are an ability to follow rhythm, an understanding of patterns, and a biological predisposition to socialize.[1] Based on this definition, the experience of dancing, whether choreographed or ecstatic, is a unique combination of factors that indicate an awareness of self, others, and something, music for instance, that is more than ourselves.

It may be true that this unique combination of factors is a lucky coincidence that evolved in a small number of species through millennia as a function for survival. Even so, I like to think of it as a gift from the divine. How incredible to be able to express our internal landscape, our feelings, thoughts, emotions, and personal stories, with our bodies. How amazing it is that we have, by circumstance, design, or anything in between, developed enough of an awareness of ourselves and our environment to create artistic outward representations of what we perceive and how we experience our existence. How beautiful that we have been gifted the means to connect with others in a way that transcends separations and accesses instincts planted deep within our subconscious.

Like dance, spirituality is a mechanism through which we experience Being. It is both a function of and a framework for relating to the world around us. It is within the realm of spirituality that we turn our focus to that which is greater than ourselves. That "greater than self" is sometimes seen as a god or a system of gods. Sometimes it is a celebration of the cycles of nature. Sometimes it is a nebulous but deeply affecting reverence for life. In many cases, admittedly for better or worse (but hopefully largely for better), the belief in the "greater than self" gives us a context through which to move and act in relation to the world around us, rooted in practices that help us to grow as individuals and connect with others in a way that touches something intrinsic in our subconsciousness. And so, dance and spirituality, though not inextricably linked in general, hold similar functions within the human experience. They both tap us into something deep within ourselves and connect us to the world around us and beyond.

For me personally, dance and spirituality *are* intrinsically linked. That connection has led me to explore and develop ways for aspects of spiritual life to be expressed or enhanced through movement practices. One major aspect in which this has manifested is in the act of giving offerings.

In many spiritual practices, the act of giving offerings to deities or to particular spirits, energies, or archetypes is fundamental to the belief system. These offerings take many forms, from prayers to acts of service to sacrifices. This can be true in secular settings as well, such as holding a gratitude journaling practice, even if it isn't dedicated to anyone or anything more than a greater idea of Life. Though offerings take many forms, many share the characteristic that they take in what is seen as being gifted to the practitioner, transform it in some way, and return it in whole or part to the perceived giver or pay it forward in a way that shows gratitude for what is gifted. It is something that is transmuted through our intention, energy, and/or work. For instance, a common offering is food placed on an altar. That food takes resources gifted from the earth and transforms them through the alchemy of cooking, which then becomes the offering given in gratitude. When water is used as an offering, it is often mixed with a drop of wine or juice, or in some cases intention and energy in place of something physical, to show that it has been considered, consecrated, and transformed, rather than returning water in its own form as a gift.

If, like me, you accept the idea that dance and the ability to do so are gifts from the gods, the creation of dance seems like a fitting offering of gratitude in return. The power inherent in dance is, perhaps with a little pun intended, very... moving. Used intentionally, the act of choreographing a devotional piece or engaging in ecstatic dance can serve as an offering in a number of ways.

- A gift for a god or spirit
- An offering of energy
- Spiritual possession or obsession practices
- Ancestor veneration
- Emulation of imagery

Each of these offerings serves a particular purpose and has unique nuances within spiritual practice.

If a practitioner is a devotee of a deity, they might create a choreographed dance with the intention of offering it as a gift to that deity, considering the energy and myths of that being and choosing sound and movement accordingly. The metaphorically alchemical act of combining the movement, music, story, energy, and intention results in a powerful, though physically intangible, offering. The piece might be performed in front of an audience, which brings attention and awareness to the goddess or god. That attention can serve as an added layer of devotional gift. The piece could also be danced alone in a private space, allowing for a deep personal connection, free from outside influence or viewership, in which the devotee can pour their heart and soul into the offering. This practice can serve as a way to deepen the relationship of the practitioner to the deity.

Though a carefully considered piece of choreography serves as a powerful gift, ecstatic dance, unplanned and without set choreography is equally effective. The purpose of ecstasis may be to offer the wild waves of kinetic energy, produced by the dance, to the gods. That energy may be earmarked for a specific purpose or it may be wholly gifted to the gods as an offering raised and directed in devotion. Ecstatic practice is unique in that it can be completely spontaneous. It is still considered and intentional but may arise at a moment's notice and be fully engaged in without preamble. It can also be fully planned as in the case of drumming and dancing around a sacred fire. Whether planned or unrehearsed, the build of energy that flows from ecstatic dance is one of the most ready forms of offering we have.

Following in the line of ecstatic dance, a practitioner could also use ecstasis and trance to offer their body for obsession or possession, the temporary use of the body by a spirit to inhabit the physical plane. This is a practice that shows up in cultures around the world and serves the purpose of offering non-physical entities a means to act in physical space or to speak with a physical voice. The practice of intentionally opening to possession is not an easy one and can easily be clouded by the ego of the practitioner who seeks it out in pursuit of power or influence. It is not to be taken lightly and should be engaged in with care, safety, and consent, particularly as it involves the offering of the practitioner's body for use by an outside entity. With all those caveats in mind however, the use of ecstatic movement to invite a spirit or deity into the body is a deeply intimate and intense gift.

In many spiritual traditions, ancestors play an important role in the greater-than-self whole. Ancestor veneration, honoring those that have walked the path before us, whether they are literal blood relatives or ancestors of spirit with whom one shares another form of kinship, is a deeply connective practice. Using dance as an offering to the ancestors can be done in the same ways as for deities and spirits, but there are also some attributes unique to the honoring of ancestors. Practicing the dance of a particular culture, respectfully and without appropriation, continues lineage and brings long-passed ancestors back to life for a moment in time. The offering in this case is the gift of carrying on the contributions of the ancestors into the present and for future generations. This is a widespread offering to those who came before along a particular path.

On a more personal level, dance might be used as an offering to a particular ancestor, calling the deceased to mind to be held in memory for a time. This may be done for the dancer alone or for an audience. It might entail the use of music or movements that remind the dancer of the person they want to honor. A dance might be a gift that the dancer would have given to the recipient when they were alive, as a child gives a drawing to a grandparent. An example specific to the dance world might be to perform the choreography of a well-known choreographer as a way to honor their memory, though in many cases that requires permission from the trusts and archives of the choreographer. In any case, the act of remembering and intentionally honoring the memory of an ancestor or a lineage when creating or performing dance can highlight the link we share through history, and even into the future for which we are ancestors to those yet to come. That act, in and of itself, is a gift both to the ancestor and to the world beyond ourselves as we celebrate the gifts passed down to us.

Somewhere between the act of creating a dance as a gift for a deity, spirit, or ancestor and the intentional offering of the body for possession, and along the same line as dancing with historical inspiration in mind, is the act of embodying positions and stances depicted in artwork as a way to connect with a particular being. We see this practice of emulation in many traditions around the world where sharing stories of the gods plays a role in culture, such as the traditional dances of India. The dancer may move through poses taken from paintings or statuary as a way to directly honor the history of the being depicted therein. They may create a new offering that blends inspiration from imagery with more modern styles of dance, perhaps becoming more abstract while still evoking traditional roots. This practice has the dual effect of opening the body to the influence of the energies and spirits, mythical heroes, and long-passed ancestors, and connecting to imagery that has generations of spiritual energy layered within it. Like most of the offerings of movement I've outlined, this gift to the gods, spirits, and ancestors can be effective as a gift in itself, an energetic offering, a form of veneration, or an invitation for possession.

This is most certainly a list made of broad brush strokes. There are infinite nuances to both dance and spirituality and so, even when we focus on one aspect, such as devotional offerings, fractals of possibility are opened and are only as limited as the imagination of the practitioner. As I said early on, dance is not inextricable from spirituality, though I might argue that spirit is intrinsically connected to dance. I am deeply grateful, in my own spiritual life, to be able to dance as a practice, to feel the magic moving through the movements as I engage with my experience of spirit and the world around me. I do have a practice of making offerings through dance and, while it is only one in a vast ocean of possible ways to connect, I feel that we have been gifted something rare with the unique set of biological traits that have allowed us to dance in the spirit of creativity, spirituality, connection, and joy. To revel in it is divine. In transforming what we have been given and giving it back, it becomes an offering of deep gratitude. Therefore, to dance is both a gift from and for the gods.

1. Kevin Laland, Clive Wilkins, Nicky Clayton, "The Evolution of Dance," *Current Biology* Volume 26 Issue 1 (2016), Pages R5-R9

Section II: Letting the Land Lead

LETTING THE
LAND LEAD

I f Movement and Magick are the threads that run through what I practice and what I teach, Letting the Land Lead is where those threads are woven into the fabric of practicality and purpose. Letting the Land Lead is an environmental dance initiative that uses movement and dance to connect participants and audiences with a deeper understanding of themselves and their relationship to the land on which they live.

Wow, that's a mouthful, even written out in a book like this! But I suppose that's what happens when the language runs through the grant writing system and elevator pitch practice over and over again.

On a more personal level, Letting the Land Lead is a simple and magical practice that opens us up to hearing messages that the land is trying to give us. It may be cliché to put it like this but clichés are so often rooted in truth; in our fast-paced world of modern conveniences, screens, and disposable everything, we are often woefully unaware of our place in, and effect on, the natural world. We have come to see ourselves as somehow divorced from Nature, and in that separation, we have forgotten that everything we are and everything we have created as humans, comes from the earth on which we live and the stars that look down on us. We have forgotten how to participate in a healthy relationship with the land.

Letting the Land Lead is my way of helping people rediscover the connection we have lost with the land in very personal ways.

It began, as you will read in the next few pages, with performances. I stumbled into the practice in graduate school and solidified it during the Covid pandemic, when dancers couldn't safely be in studio spaces, spending time, instead, engaging with dance outdoors. As the concept grew and I realized the impact that might be possible with outdoor, environmentally-focused and themed dance performances, I started to connect with land trusts and conservation spaces to bring awareness to their work with my performances. At the same time, I began teaching the process in workshops at spiritual festivals and as added bonuses to the live performances I was orchestrating. I even hosted a small retreat to develop and teach the practice over the course of a long weekend.

More recently, I was invited to teach Letting the Land Lead as a guest presenter and choreographer at a university, working with a professor of aquatic research in the science department, along with the dance department, as well as artistic and musical collaborators, to create rich, multifaceted performances, highlighting the land around the school and the research of the professor and students. Through that experience, my collaborators and I were able to speak about the work at an environmental conference, with a very warm response I might add. Bit by bit the work continues to grow!

On the macrocosmic level, my dream for Letting the Land Lead is that it will be a self-sustaining initiative - an organization of choreographers, dancers, planners, designers, fundraisers, producers, and public representatives that has the means to support the needs of environmental protection efforts. In the microcosm of this work, it is much simpler. Letting the Land Lead centers around a practice of learning about ourselves and moving with the land. We start by going inward and exploring our own movement language. We then take that movement to the land and allow the land to change it. Letting the land lead us in that way helps us to better understand the subtle, and sometimes not-so-subtle, signals that we are always receiving from the earth.

That is the process. It is meditative and quietly spiritual. It is a welcoming and approachable doorway for people to connect with themselves and the environment through the language of movement. It helps us to be in better relationship with the world around us.

Without further ado, I invite you to read about how Letting the Land Lead began and how to try it for yourself.

The Dance is calling!

The Seed of Letting the Land Lead

Movement I : Partnering

I joined the Tango Club when I was in college. I was a dance major, so it made sense as an extra-curricular, but honestly, I only joined because I had a crush on a guy and it was an enticing way to spend time with him. Tango is, after all, one of the most romantic dances there is. There is a closeness, an understanding between the partners as they move across the floor. Each partner, lead and follow, knows what they are doing. They are aware of themselves first, knowing how they might move and respond. They've learned steps from generations of dancers before them, developing an inner knowledge of how the techniques work, and why.

When two dancers come together, knowing the techniques and styles for themselves, they can then open to a deep awareness of one another. They communicate without speaking, almost magically, as they follow the patterns of the dance. Movements are seamless statements and responses, the lead guiding a flowing path across the floor and the follower ending that path in a flourish that adds beauty and finesse. They are able to play and express, showing off a little for whomever might be watching. But really, it's for them, inside the dance.

While my crush didn't last terribly long, I did learn a lot about being a good partner in the dance. It requires a few things. First of all, you have to be aware of yourself. Of course it helps to know some steps, but, even as a beginner, it's possible to follow someone who knows what they're doing if you're aware of yourself.

Then you need to be able to listen and respond, to communicate. The follower must be able to listen to the lead. If the lead is strong and aware, listening with the body and following is not only easy but joyful and beautiful, as much to watch as it is to dance. And the lead also listens, feeling the edges of the movements and responses of their partner. The whole is greater than either could do on their own when all the parts are put into practice well.

This short time dancing tango, with all its long-lasting impact, was also yet a small flourish in the whole of my dance training. Throughout my training in ballet, modern, and post-modern dance, I learned ways to express and communicate as a soloist, in groups large and small, and as a partner. In ballet, a structure was given, set familiar movements that spoke a kind of language with which a dancer or choreographer could create a story or moving poem. In modern and post-modern dance, exploration was key. Anything and everything could become dance and so it was the intention of a movement and the way the dancer filled it with feeling that spoke its meaning. And then there was contact improvisation. This extemporaneous sharing of creative space with other dancers taught me to trust in an unknown partner, sharing weight, performing seemingly spectacular feats, and having deep and intimate silent conversations while trusting in my own ability to catch myself should the need arise.

Each skill, filling out familiar and prescribed movement

vocabulary, creating something new from any source of inspiration, and especially the ability to communicate between bodies without words, all contributed to the whole of what was to become my work, both in the dance world and beyond it.

Movement II: The Serendipitous Seed

It was years later when I was a graduate student in Scotland that I began to understand how these principles work in the greater scope of things. I was in a practice-focused intensive master's program at the Glasgow School of Art, deepening my performance practice as a dancer. Over the course of the year, I struggled to connect with the land, having arrived in this place that I'd dreamed of for most of my life with the romantic assumptions I had built over years of idolizing Celtic art, folklore and magic. My goal at school was to create spiritual dance pieces that were inspired by the land and myths I had so idolized.

The land was everything I dreamed it would be; stunning, striking, melancholic, inspiring, and I loved every moment of exploring it...

But no matter what I did, I felt stuck. Sure, I made some pieces of art that I was very happy with over the year, but somehow, I just couldn't get past the wall to real Connection, the experience of being able to feel the energy, even spirit, of the land. I was missing the sense of understanding and flow that I had developed through my spiritual practice with the land I lived on at home. Admittedly, I had nearly two decades to connect with that land, becoming familiar with its ebbs and flows of energy and magic, but I made the naïve assumption that I would be able to simply plug myself into the spiritual landscape in Scotland and begin to create masterworks of magical art. This was not the case.

As the year was drawing to a close and my classmates and I were preparing for our final exhibitions, I had the idea to lean into the Celtic concept of the Three Realms — Land, Sea and Sky — to create my master's thesis work. I choreographed movement and enlisted the help of a friend in the moving image track of the program to go with me and film the movement out in the dramatic Scottish landscape. I chose three places to connect with the Realms: the forest near Loch Lomond for Land, the seaside at Largs on the western coast for Sea, and the top of a "hill" (I'd call it a small mountain) in Campsie Glen for Sky.

We went to the mountain first. The bus ride to Campsie Glen from Buchanan Street Station in Glasgow lasted nearly an hour. Along the way we settled all the details for our filming; the climb, the shots, the movement. It had been a relatively warm early summer day, until, as it does in Scotland, the day turned cold and rainy as the bus carried us to the Glen. We climbed the hill and made it to the top, which was no small feat in and of itself. Over the course of the year exploring the Scottish landscape, I'd begun to call it "the land of optical illusion" because the muted browns and greens of the vegetation and stones that blanket nearly every vista invariably tricked me into believing that any distance between two points was shorter than it truly was.

When we finally reached the summit, already cold and wind-whipped, I found another shock waiting for me. From years of climbing mountains at home in the northeastern United States, I had anticipated arriving at the top of the hill to find grassy or rocky terrain, perhaps wet but easy enough to dance on. What I found instead could only be described as wetlands, with shrubs and mossy ground, pitted and uneven and, in most places, drowned in water up to my calves. Of all the things I thought possible, I never imagined there would be a marsh on top of a mountain. There was no way I could dance as I had planned!

But I had to do something! We didn't trek all that way to go home with an empty camera.

I stared around for a few minutes, at a loss as to what to do. It really was strikingly beautiful, the clouds and wind providing a mood that the Brontë sisters would envy. The sky roiled grey as far as the eye could see over a stark but deeply emerald green and russet brown landscape. The dry willowy grasses, bowing to the insistent wind, were webbed intermittently with the shorn cast-offs of drenched wool from the sheep that had grazed nearby when the day hadn't yet been so dreary, the effect of which was to make areas of the ground appear to be cast over in large cob webs. Despite the perfectly gothic mood, my body, shaking from the damp chill, begged me to go back down the hill, climb back on the heated bus, and get back to a hot shower and warm clothes as soon as possible. I almost gave in.

Instead, I let myself be taken by what was available to me. I changed into the costume I brought, a thin linen shirt the same steely gray as the clouds and linen trousers that blended with the sandy hue of the land. Out of my bag I pulled a tattered piece of fabric that I had dyed with rust, giving it a similar hue to the stony path. Then I found a place to plant my bare feet, ankle deep in frigid rain water sequestered among the shrubs and mosses. I let go my expectations of the dance I had choreographed and instead held the fabric aloft to catch the wind. I gave everything over to the sky. I danced in place, moving with the wind and rain, shaking and sniffling but losing myself to everything around me.

It was miserable and it was glorious. The intense wind became my dance partner, pulling at the fabric, wrapping me in it to create haunting images of my face encased in a shroud, then flying free, moving me along with it. I was a ghost and a gust of wind, a shrub and an explorer lost on the moors. When the dance was over and I came fully back to myself, the cold took over and I gave into the need and desire to go back home and be warm again.

In that moment on the hilltop, I felt it, the Connection I sought that had eluded me. I didn't understand it entirely yet but I knew that something had shifted. I had let go and the land had responded by offering something more than I could imagine myself. The images my friend and I created together with the land were unplanned, unexpected, and exactly what the land was calling for and offering me. This piece is still one of my favorite creations out of all the work I've done.

A few weeks later in the forest, an hour's train ride north-west of Glasgow, looking over the southern end of Loch Lomond, I explored this process again. This time I knew that I needed to let myself fall into the land as I had learned on the mountain top. Dancing barefoot on twigs and pinecones, sharp edges taking the occasional bite into the sensitive skin of my feet, forced a very deliberate pace of movement. I explored the forest floor with care, communicating with the earth on its terms, not my own. I climbed a mossy tree that had fallen and rested at an angle, holding tightly onto the slippery, smooth, and wet bark with both fingers and toes so as not to slip or lose balance. I played like this for a time, learning what was possible within that delicate frame of movement. I experimented with the sounds of the leaves and twigs under foot and did my best to imitate the steps of a deer. I ran along a path, darting between trees and jumping over fallen branches. Still, my movements were considered and deliberate, more mobile than on the marshy mountain but careful nonetheless.

At the shore however, on a beautiful warm and sunny day, I was able to dance with wild abandon. With nothing to impede my movement or inform particular caution, I threw myself along the beach, reveling in the flat grey sands of the western shoreline of Scotland and gazing out towards the isles in the Firth of Clyde. Donning my costume of linen again as I had twice before, I splashed through silvery tide pools reflecting the sky and my movements in their shallow depths. The salt water flew from my feet as I swirled like a drafter's compass, drawing circles in the wet sand. I jumped and flew and glided over the rippled sand and shimmering water as I let fun and freedom be my guide. Then I waded out into the gentle waves, knee-deep and welcomingly warm for a surprising distance. I danced there, letting the water gently move me, slowing my rapid human movements with its natural resistance but also encouraging an exploration of its calm push and pull and soft support. The simple quietude of the ocean on that day felt like an invitation, both to sink into the hush of the day and to rebel against it in defiant playfulness. Finally, when my frolicking energy had ebbed, I let myself lay fully back into the water, giving in and soaking my costume and the rest of me completely, filming the final shots of the project.

Each location had informed a particular way of moving and had guided me to show its personality as well as my own, creating something unique to those moments. The final project, a triptych of five-minute videos projected into the arms of a triskele, a triple spiral ubiquitous around much of the world but very prevalent in Celtic imagery, showed three very different, yet intrinsically linked, moving images of the land and my exploration of it. Together, they represented what I hadn't been able to find before I came up against that first unexpected experience on the top of the mountain: a deep Connection with the land. I realized that up until I gave into what the land was offering me instead of trying to impose my own plans and expectations, I hadn't been listening. I hadn't been a good dance partner. I had explored, hiked, trudged, traveled, boated, ritualized, and even danced in ecstasy on the land in this place that was my new and temporary home, but I was searching for something I wanted and expected to find, not listening to and discovering what was really there.

That's when I began to learn how to let the land lead.

Movement III: Letting the Land Lead

It took time for the lessons to settle in but slowly I started to integrate what I had experienced. I began to understand my own language of communication. For quite some time, likely since I had studied dance in college, movement had been my way of relating to the world. Over years of studying and expressing through my body's own language, words had become secondary to deep physical understanding. As I put that way of understanding into practice, it became clear that, in moving with the land, it is possible to discern what nature is saying. However, that can only happen by deeply knowing our own method of communicating and then opening to what the land has to offer through that lens. In learning that, the lessons from my days dancing tango began to flood back, and they became even more important. We must be both self-aware and empathetic towards others to be good dance partners. The same holds true when we relate to the world beyond dance. By knowing ourselves first, understanding our inner language, we can become sensitive and compassionate partners to the world around us as we move through it.

As Letting the Land Lead has continued to grow and develop, it has become a simple but deeply affecting practice. At its heart is a technique that weaves in a great deal of what I learned in my days as a dance major and everything that I picked up roaming the Scottish countryside. We begin by going inward, moving in ways that help us to know ourselves better. Then we begin to focus outward so that we know how to listen with every part of ourselves. It really is simple, I cannot express that enough, but in its simplicity is a way to reach that sense of connection that so many of us lose because we spend so much time disconnecting from the world.

Since the seed of Letting the Land Lead serendipitously planted itself in my life, the work has wound its way from my master's thesis, through an online dance video that I created for a choreography challenge early in the Covid shutdown, to live and online performances in partnership with conservation spaces and land trusts, and on to teaching workshops and classes, and even a small but very enthusiastic retreat. It has even reached the hallowed halls of higher education, working with a university to integrate environmental science and the arts. And it is still very much growing.

Letting the Land Lead is still young, but each time I engage in the practice in any of its many iterations, I notice how letting go and trusting the process of going inward to then relate outward again always makes me just a little bit more aware. That, in turn, makes me just a little bit better at being in good relationship with the world around me. My hope is that, as this initiative continues to grow, we're able to affect audiences and participants, dancers and students, and anyone who is drawn to wonder what it's all about, so that they too can learn to listen inward and then be better partners with the land. In time, I hope that we can bring about enough change to see the world and our environment a noticeable bit better off because of what Letting the Land Lead has to teach us.

How to Let the
Land Lead

A t its core, Letting the Land Lead is a practice that helps us to understand our own inner language in order to help us better understand our connection to the land on which we live.

This practice is simple.

1. **We start by going inward.**

Letting the Land Lead starts inside, literally, as in, indoors. We begin in a studio or indoor space that's generally conducive to movement and dance.

It also starts inside figuratively, exploring our inner landscape, how our bodies want to move, how they want to express and communicate.

I'd love for you to be able to experience this practice as well so here is an outline to explore, if you like. Know, as you read and try it, that there is no wrong way to do it. Anybody, any body, can engage with this practice regardless of movement experience or physical ability. It can be done as a full-scale dance jam, with a wide range of movement and dance, or take place more quietly, seated, lying down, or whatever your body needs whenever you enter into the practice. No one way is more effective than any other, precisely because it exists to connect us to the present moment as we are. Try it at home or in a studio. Try it out in nature. Try it with music and without. Try it alone or with others. Please play and explore! Here is how it goes...

Close your eyes and bring your focus to your breathing, allowing yourself to slow down. At first, just notice. Then, connect with your heartbeat for a few breaths. Just notice again. Then, let your mind wander through your body, and again, yes, just notice.

What is your body telling you? Your energy? Your emotions?

As your mind wanders through your body, say "yes" to any places that are calling for attention. Move, bend, twist, stretch, squeeze, massage, tense, relax, all as your body is asking. (This is also a warm-up, cleverly disguised as a meditation.) Allow for this to become a dance of saying "yes" to all the things your body is asking for in the moment. You should find that one movement informs another; the bend of a knee informs the roll of a hip and, in turn, the curve of the spine and then the turn of the head and so on. Let this exploration continue and build for as long as you like.

This is your Internal Conversation.

Then, still with your eyes closed, turn your focus outward, listening and feeling, sensing what's around you. Notice things that catch your attention in your space and let them inform your movement. Hear the sounds of the room, the music, the air system, the other people, if there are any, breathing and moving. Notice the weight of your body on your feet or however you are supported, shifting as your movement continues. Notice how the air around you and the fabric of your clothes feel on your skin. See the light behind your eyelids. Let these points of interest move you. Eventually, when you feel called to, open your eyes and continue to move, adding the sense of sight to the many things that are calling you to move.

This is your External Conversation.

Now, do both at once. Let the External Conversation and the Internal Conversation inform each other. Let the movement of your body and breath cause you to move and notice something in your surroundings which then informs another movement; the color of light coming from a lamp tilts your head which moves your shoulders leading you into a bend which causes you to notice the texture of the floor and so on. Let this go on as long as you like.

Eventually, let yourself come to stillness. Again, just notice. What did you notice? What feels different now compared to when you began?

You can stop here and just let it be or go on to the rest of the practice.

2. **Then we set movement.**

I always hesitate to call this part "choreography" because that word can be intimidating to people who don't consider themselves "dancers." We are, however, at this point, effectively choreographing a movement piece.

There are so many ways to set movement into repeatable phrases. For Letting the Land Lead, there is no right way except that the movement should be familiar and repeatable to those executing it. For some, that may be a fully-choreographed ballet or modern dance. For others, it may be a yoga flow designed with a theme in mind. For some, it may be a repeatable pattern of walking steps. It could even live in the realm of improvisation, as long as the style is clear to those moving.

One simple way of setting movement for the purposes of this practice, is to move back into your internal and external conversations and try to remember, movement by movement, a short, repeatable phrase, like a sentence of movements strung together. How did your body want to move? Did you notice any movements that just felt right as you were doing them? Build from there and create something that is recognizable to you. It only needs to be a few seconds long to work.

Then it's time to really Let the Land Lead.

3. **Then we take it to the land.**

Once we have a set bit of movement, even the smallest phrase, we can take it into an outdoor space and try it. The land will naturally cause us to move differently than we did in a studio or indoor space. What was a turn might become a body twist when we're moving on grass because turning on grass would rip up the soil, something we definitely want to avoid in this practice of connecting with the land. Running and jumping are tricky over tree roots and so these movements may need to be done slowly. Improvisation even becomes more deliberate when the terrain is uncertain. We'll notice how these movements change, how our body language changes, informed by the land, when we're really familiar with how our own bodies are speaking.

As we engage with the Inner and Outer Conversations and our set phrasework, we have the opportunity to let the familiarity of our own movements guide us into surprising moments of awareness with our environment. Once, while teaching this process in a workshop, I created a phrase during which I suddenly encountered a beam of afternoon sunlight in my cupped hands. From there I saw the earliest colors of the changing autumn leaves as I followed the beam upward with my movement. The pointing branches then led me to see the movement of the clouds in the early autumn breeze.

As we notice these beautiful details in conjunction with the changes that the land makes to our movement, we begin to hear what the land has to offer us, what it is saying. We might begin to feel how dry and dusty a path through the forest is when the season has been unusually devoid of rain. We may notice the banks of a local river flooding after too many storms. We may see, for the first time, a type of flower or fungus growing that we've never taken the time to notice before. Perhaps we may even see new changes to the landscape we've been familiar with for years, like the sudden falling of a tree or a change in the bend of a riverbed.

More than anything though, when we engage with this practice over time, we begin to notice patterns. We see cycles of the seasons changing from year to year. We take note of the shorter winters, longer wet seasons, and hotter summers. We begin to notice new plants growing after a flood where they've never been before or an absence of familiar plants and animals in places they used to frequent. We also build a deeper awareness of our own patterns, our cycles that shift and change with how we relate to the world around us. We begin to notice all of these things, and the Internal and External Conversations, the techniques that we practice in the studio, begin to blend subtly into daily life. Soon, the practice becomes second nature and we are in quiet but constant conversation with the world around us. We engage in noticing what's going on around us every day, and more importantly, we begin to ask questions which lead us to understand the land better.

All of this is Letting the Land Lead. But deep at the heart of Letting the Land Lead is the simple practice of

1. Going Inward
2. Setting Movement
3. Taking It to the Land

and that's really all we need to do.

Section III: Dancing with Giants

DANCING WITH GIANTS

T he work and the path I have embarked on with the
Giants came as a surprise. It arose out of an unexpected need and a discovery within that necessity.
Now that I'm here walking it though, the path seems like such
a natural trajectory, stemming from my spiritual and magickal
practice and my dance work in relation to the environment
and Nature.

Like all the sections of this book, this introduction is only
a doorway to the deeper work yet to come. My experience with
the Giants is relatively new, a statement which becomes an
incredible understatement if we consider the time scale of a
Giant, but we'll get into that shortly. What I am presenting
here is only the beginning of my research and exploration, but
within this *Prelude* I am offering and introducing a little bit
about how I came to walk this path seeking out the Giants,
and a very little bit of the reason.

I see our relationship with the Giants as one going back to
the beginning of our species and beyond. It is ever-evolving.
My stories will tell you why that's important, and there will be
more to come, but it is that relationship that is at the heart of

Dancing with Giants. For now, I will simply say that the stories I am telling here are true, both in a literal sense, and an allegorical one. I invite you to approach these essays and stories in whatever way calls to you. I hope that by offering this beginning, you may find that you're similarly called to meet a Giant. You may even realize that you know some Giants already.

Maybe you'll join the dance!

WHO ARE THE GIANTS?

Giants feature in myth, legend, and fairy tales in cultures all over the world. Maybe it's in our nature as humans to fear or revere something that is unfathomably larger than ourselves. Maybe our imaginings and personifications of the spirits we perceive in nature and culture drive us to include the Giants ubiquitously in our mythological backgrounds. When we distill the tropes from the world of myth and then take a look around us with a keen eye, it is possible to view Giants as they really are.

When I began my exploration of the Giants, I asked some trusted friends, who are long-time practitioners of Heathenry, what their opinions of the Giants are, as they feature heavily, and not without complexity, in Norse and Germanic myth. The answer that most struck me was that the Giants represent natural forces that are deeply and unapologetically themselves. "You cannot ask a Storm to be anything other than itself." With that answer, I began to understand why the Giants are often vilified in stories and, in myths, are often imprisoned or controlled by the Gods. In ages past, prior to our modern sense of separation from and power over nature, the idea of the gods as a civilizing force, holding the powers of nature at bay, would be deeply appealing. But the Giants are complex. They are uncontrollable and potentially destructive, but they are also powerfully creative. There is so much more to say about this relationship but that could fill another book entirely.

For the purposes of this *Prelude*, let me introduce you to the Giants as I have begun to see them.

Giants are, by nature, giant. They are beings that exist on a scale far beyond what we understand as human beings. This is the case both in size and in time. They are massive beings that live for millennia or, equally intensely, in the span of mere hours. They are the spirits of mountains or full mountain ranges, storms and hurricanes, wildfires, islands and land masses, oceans, and indeed, the Earth itself as a whole. They can represent Time, Creation, or Destruction. They are also Ideas, egregores, collective thought forms that take on lives of their own. There is an intangible but palpable sense of being-ness that indicates the presence of a Giant.

Encountering a Giant can be subtle or surprising, gentle or intimidating, but it is, almost always, an awe-inspiring experience. Very often, if you don't miss it completely because of its enormity beyond a scale we can perceive, meeting a Giant happens suddenly and very obviously, such as turning a bend on a trail and seeing the view of an imposing mountain all at once. It may be difficult to pinpoint exactly how you know it is a Giant that you are seeing but, at the same time, you know it to be true. The feeling of recognition that washes over in that moment is pervasive. That is a Giant.

Speaking to the Giants is a bit less obvious. Like encountering any beyond-human entity, or indeed any person that speaks an unfamiliar language, it is necessary to learn common ground to reach understanding. In the case of the Giants, in order to engage with them, they must be met on their own terms. A mountain may be able to teach a great deal, but it has existed for hundreds of thousands of years and its language requires patience to hear. The Giant of a storm system, on the other hand, may live only a few hours or even minutes, and poses very real destructive and dangerous potential. It must be interacted with safely and within its timeframe to be understood.

There is a great deal we can learn from Giants. Their natural and unwavering truth-of-self is a powerful lesson on its own. But as spirits of nature, they can also tell us a great deal about the world. The personalities of hurricanes and wildfires, for instance, are, even now, telling us that the climate is changing. The vastness of a desert Giant can teach us how to move and shift like the sand in the wind. The stillness of a mountain Giant can teach us an inner quiet that weathers change.

But more than what we can learn from them, Giants are simply themselves. They have existed and will continue to exist far beyond our own span as humans. Perhaps that is an important perspective to hold as this work unfolds, that we are so much smaller than these colossal entities. My own sense is that the Giants of myth have been imprisoned too long, shackled by the "advancements" of "civilization" to the point of forcing their way out and breaking free in the form of massive, destructive weather events. I believe that shows a deep need for us to examine our relationship with the Giants, and indeed with Nature itself, with a critical eye. Whether we learn from their myths and stories from cultures around the world and ages past, or directly from the source, meeting them in person, I feel that it is important to find out the truths of these Giants and who they are, coming to understand how to live in better relationship with them and the spirits of Nature.

Dancing with Giants

*H*urricane to hit New England coast. May travel as far inland as Central Massachusetts. High winds expected. Trees down. Mobile homes will be destroyed.

That last bit caught my attention. Not a great notification to receive from your weather app if you live in a mobile home. I did.

Hurricanes in Massachusetts are few and far between enough, but one that could hit as far inland as my little hamlet with a force enough to destroy my home?! What was I supposed to do with information like that? It's not as if we keep plywood laying around to board up windows like my family in Florida would, not that boarding up windows would have been enough if "mobile homes will be destroyed" was the warning of the day.

The storm was to hit the next day. It was building force out in the Atlantic and was slated to make landfall sometime before midday. I had been visiting a friend when the notifications showed up. I moved slowly, keeping an eye on the weather reports as they continued to roll in. Eventually I decided it was time to make my way home to the house I shared with my mother, who was blessedly away for an extended period and would miss whatever was about to happen, to start making what preparations I could. There really wasn't much I could do except to take all of my mother's knick knacks off the patio and lock them in the shed, preventing the resin angel from literally taking wing should the cataclysmic storm truly arrive in full force.

And then there was nothing left to do but hunker down for the night.

The previous day had been sunny and hot, but waking on the day of the storm felt drastically different. The sky was grey and gloomy, honestly my preferred type of weather, but much less comforting when it portends the possible destruction of my home. The wind had noticeably picked up, blowing sharp gusts with increasing frequency and remaining fairly steady in between. Each growing breath of the storm sent shivers of worry through my chest as the voice of the wind turned from an insistent shushing to a whistling moan around and through the vinyl siding of the house.

Overnight I had considered what else I could do to protect myself and shore up my home. An unfortunate lack of solution echoed silently through my mind. I considered the possibility of getting out of there until it was all over, come what may. I can't put my finger on why exactly; maybe it was a sense of inconvenience for myself and whoever might host me, maybe it was some false sense of control in staying, but leaving didn't seem like the best option, despite the potential danger. I decided I would stay.

With that decision made, the only thing left for me to do to safeguard my home was magick.

That morning, as the storm spun its way toward shore, I

made the calculated decision to go to one of my magickal places in the woods not far from where I lived, a place from which I could look out over the valley where my home and many others sat waiting to endure their fate. Admittedly, I had little to no plan. I simply knew where I needed to go and I trusted that something would come to me once I arrived.

It was a nervous climb to a potentially dangerous vantage point. I'd climbed it often but in the growing wind and spitting rain I was less sure-footed than usual. But up I went, the branches whipping above me, the rubble and rocks sliding under my boots. The anticipatory thrum of nerves, tingling and rippling from within my chest, through my arms and legs with every new surge of wind, threatened to pull me back along the path, back to the car, and home to some version of relative safety, but I didn't listen. I forged onward, feeling that it was necessary to offer a real show of effort behind any magick I was about to do to give it as much potential power as possible.

Picking my way carefully over slippery roots and making my way around the bends and curves of the trail as my legs burned from the sharp incline, I made my way towards the ledge overlooking the eastern vista. I moved carefully and gingerly, using every ounce of awareness my training as a dancer afforded me, sneaking as close to the edge as I dared in the gale, which is to say not very, and held onto a well-rooted tree for assurance.

Looking out over the valley that morning was the first time I really understood what a Giant truly is. That sight changed my relationship with them forever.

I had seen them before, land giants, spirits of Nature, land wights, genii loci. All giants are impressive in their stature and energy, but those I had seen previously were, in a way, personable and relatable. A grandmother tree deep in the forest is a beauty to behold and carries a powerful energy; a boulder or stone outcropping that is enspirited with the energy of a land giant may be imposing and intimidating. Still, these spirits often feel approachable and comprehensible within a scope a human might understand.

These Giants were different. Before me, as tall as moving mountains, were Giants made of cloud, vast, towering, and gray. They were walking, yes, very clearly walking step by step across the valley in droves. Watching this parade of nimbus beings, a thousand feet tall, parading across the landscape toward who knows where, driven on by the winds of the approaching storm, I sensed within them an energy, a consciousness even, that dwarfed my own. They were so clearly alive that I felt as if, at any moment, one of these clouds might suddenly turn against the wind, seeing me, and move contrary to its natural path to confront me if it so chose, not that a being as miniscule as I am would warrant such attention from ones so vast.

Something in me shifted instantly. I was in awe and, at the same time, I was struck with an unexpected understanding. Suddenly seeing these Giants as they marched across the hills and valleys gave me an appreciation of the magnitude and vivacity that they hold. These beings are the ones the myths are written about. They are fearsome because they are massive, powerful, and beyond our scope of comprehension, as we live in the bodies that we do. In comparison, we are small, finite, delicate, and short-lived. That is not to say that we cannot experience the wonder of these beings, but unlike the tangible, textured occurrences of human life, the only way to comprehend the hugeness of a Giant is to let go into the experience of it. That was what standing on the ledge in the burgeoning bluster of the storm forced me to do, simply acknowledge and be with the Giants.

With this new awareness, I turned away from the cliff edge. There was a place I knew a little farther back in the forest off of an old, lesser-used trail. It was a sort of stone circle, in the sense that it was a roughly circular gathering of stones that had likely been deposited by a glacier a hundred thousand years ago or more. It seemed like as good a place as any to work magick, though I still didn't have any clear plan. Even as I hiked away from the ledge, the knee-buckling fear I naturally associated with the thought of a slip or trip over the edge refused to subside. My heart was pounding, more than any fear of heights would normally cause. It dawned on me that, in seeing the Giants striding on the wind, the reality of the possible magnitude of the hurricane was crashing into me. I was scared and I had to hurry.

I wound my way through the bushes, each catch of a twig on my clothes pulling me closer to the edge of frenzy. When I reached the stones, well-tucked into the woods, I worked to quiet the frantic whirring of my mind and opened myself to what needed to be done in order to somehow petition the storm to spare the vulnerable houses and people in its path. Unthinking, I began to sway and pace, building up the rocking wave that beats at the edges of regular thought and coaxes the mind into a state of magickal flow, like the beating of the wind against the forested hill. With my head rolled back towards the sky, I began to speak.

"Please, great Giant of the storm, don't destroy my home and the homes of the people in your path. Please let your energy be spent safely, without harm. Please move and shift and dissipate."

As I spoke and the words began to pour from me, it began to feel as if a great figure, taller than the trees, was watching me through the circle of branches above the clearing. Being a dancer, I have felt the free abandon of dancing alone in a studio, no eyes to see me. I have also felt the thrill, and potential scrutiny, of an entire auditorium full of onlookers. Though I could see nothing more than the circle of cloudy sky through the trees while I paced and rocked and chanted, the sensation of being watched tingled across my skin, pounding through my blood as surely as if I was on stage, and I knew that I had an audience. I could sense just one set of eyes, but those eyes looked down through the trees from a great height, and I felt the Giant crouching down to watch. Maybe it heard me calling. Maybe it was just the energy of the storm that had come to inhabit the land for a brief time, watching in fascination as this little human, dumb enough to be out in the path of the storm, wandered around the forest erratically. Either way, I knew that I was being watched, and so I continued.

"Giant of the storm, I am just a little witch! I am only one, but the need is great! Please do not harm us here in this land! Please move and disperse! May the energy of your storm find a use in another way!"

I went on like this for a while, building the prayer, layering words as I swayed and paced. Somewhere within my chant as I repeated "I am just a small being, just a witch," a shift occurred and a new plea began to weave into the tapestry of supplication. "I have little to offer, I don't know what to do," I declared, with the knowledge that I must give something as an offering rising to the surface of my entreaty.

"Dance." A deep voice that rumbled like thunder pulsed within my mind.

I had danced in the woods before as a performance and as a practice in my magick, but this felt different and more dire. I gave in. I listened as the wind blew gusts through the trees, feeling them buffet my already-swaying body and letting it lead me. The sway of my spine increased as I let the command course through my body. My arms wheeled overhead, guiding me to look up to where I felt the Giant gazing earthward. Then I crashed down, kneeling and throwing the force of my hands towards the rotting blanket of leaves beneath my feet, spreading my fingers like mycelial networks. Energy followed my hands up from the earth as I rose again in a wave and swirled in the blowing wind. My dance grew as I reacted to the sounds of the forest in the storm and the gusts of my own breath. The scent of rich earth in the rain, the petrichor of years of life fallen from the branched arms of the trees above me, wafted through my nose while I huffed and panted with the growing fervor of my magick. The soil softened the sounds of my footfalls, though at times a twig or stick would snap loudly, offering intermittent percussion. I lost myself to the dance. I had never been quite so desperate for my magick to work before.

I continued my chanting as the waves of movement and magick flowed through me. "I am just a small witch but I offer this dance to you, Giants! Please let this storm subside! Protect our homes and our lives! Let no harm be done!"

I don't know how long it lasted, this dance-prayer for my unseen audience. In actuality, it probably wasn't all that long because, at some point in my magickal ecstasy, the knowledge that I still needed to go home and make sure there was nothing more to be done crept back into the underlayer of my aware-ness. I was still at least somewhat aware of the humbling fact of my mortality, dancing around in the woods as a hurricane was blowing. The sheer number of possible widow-maker branches overhead was more than enough to rein me back in.

My movement slowed, my heaving breaths continuing as the concern over the safety of my house sidled its way back into my mind. I closed my Working, repeating my petitions once more and giving thanks to the land and to the storm and the Giants that had become so clear to me that day. I left the energy of the dance, a great deal of it if I felt it correctly, to the

Giant as my offering, the movement and improvised choreography hopefully serving as enough of a gift. I made my way carefully but quickly back to the trail to scramble down the rocky cliff path.

When I reached the top of the rocky descent, the boulders laid out below me, I paused briefly in my rush. As I stepped down onto the first landing of stone, grasping a tree for support, I heard the same thunderous voice declare, "You are Stormdancer." The proclamation coursed through me like a lightning bolt, raising the hair on my arms as if the air was charged with electricity. As I remember it, the moment was paradoxical, both undeniably consequential and yet somewhat anticlimactic while my focus was trained on getting down the path and making my way home. In some ways it was subtle as the first quiet rumblings of thunder, as if I had imagined it, and in other ways it crashed into me like a wave. The gray sheen of the wet stones of the path, my hand on the smooth bark of a tree, the cold dripping sweat soaking my clothes after the ecstatic dance, are all imprinted on my memory of that moment as it sank into my being. Stormdancer was both a name and a call to action. It was not only a label given in recognition of something I had done, some magick I had worked while very literally dancing in the storm, but a charge to continue to dance with storms, with the Giants. The Name was both a gift and something to grow into. I paused in gratitude, feeling honored to be given a Name through this Work.

And yet the wind and rain were still bombarding the valley and the side of a rocky cliff was no place to linger. I made my way back to my car, continuing my prayers to the storm with my new-found wonder and appreciation of the realities of the Giants.

Shortly after I returned home, it was all over. No more than an hour after I offered my dance to the Giant in the windblown woods, the clouds parted and the winds ebbed.

The summer sun was once again bright and warm, the heat softened by a light breeze. The sounds of the day shifted from the howling of the wind back to the hum of vehicles on the road just south of the house. The stream nearby burbled and the birds went back to flitting around the awning over the parked car. It was almost hard to accept the drastic transformation. It felt as if there had never been a storm at all.

And yet there had been a storm, and Giants, and I was left with a new Name and a new door to open and explore. I am in this exploration now as I write this story down, not knowing where it will lead, working to build a relationship with the Giants and what they represent as spirits of Nature.

To be clear, I am not claiming sole responsibility for the path of the storm. Far from it. I do not control the weather, that should go without saying. I am, as I said, just a small witch, and Giants cannot be controlled. That is not the nature of Nature. I did learn much later that the storm was not entirely without casualty, with a great deal of flooding and widespread power outages throughout New England, though thank goodness no reported deaths. However, it was a gratifying surprise to read reports saying that the storm had dissipated much more quickly than anticipated, just after the timeframe of my dance in the woods. I have to believe that we, as workers of magick in whatever form, including those that may call it something different, can and should find our own ways to relate to the Giants of the land.

Our relationship to Nature is changing as the climate shifts and we are experiencing unprecedented events on a regular basis. There are Giants within many of these natural phenomena; the hurricanes and wildfires that ravage more of the land every year; the melting ice at the poles of the earth, the swing and flow of currents as they shift and change deep within the ocean. We have to be able to dance with these Giants. It is going to take time to learn, but we cannot learn if we do not take those first few steps, and in those first few steps, we need to show a willingness to give offerings of ourselves. Without that, we cannot even begin. I believe that this dance, learned from our ancestors and taught to generations to come, who will change it as their world changes, will heal our relationship with the Giants. Dancing with Giants is the way we come back to ourselves and heal our world.

THE SECOND DANCE

I t was during a ceremonial ritual for the sun.

I am not, by nature, a Ceremonial Magician. Though familiar in concept, that type of magick is foreign to me in practice. My magick is rooted, eclectic, intuitive, and a little wild. This ritual was opulent, calculated, ecstatic within a mathematical container. I was intrigued and open to the experience but also unsure of what might be waiting for me in the small, tightly-packed room.

The space filled quickly with excited participants. We took up every cranny like water in a vessel, squeezing into nooks and alcoves, forming a circle to focus at the center. The sheer mass of people only served to intensify the build of energy.

I was nervous, being relatively unfamiliar with this type of working, and my apprehension peaked when the doors were closed. The ritualists informed us that once the container of the circle was closed, no one was to leave until the end except in the case of an emergency. They gave us one last opportunity to opt out. A small part of me whispered that it might be better if I just left. A few people did shuffle toward the door but otherwise there was a great deal of rapt anticipation, made evident by the hushed whispers and eager murmurs. And so it began.

I cannot, and wouldn't if I could, detail the ceremony itself, both out of respect for tradition and a desire to maintain the sacred Mystery. Suffice it to say that its intricately executed structure formed a powerful vessel for the ritual work. Within it, power built as chants were intoned. The participants moved and swayed as the current surged and flowed. I danced, though cramped in place, as is my usual way of connecting to the power of magic and ritual.

Despite the esoteric beauty of the ritual, enough certainly to have left an impression, I am not exaggerating when I say that I cannot remember much about what occurred. As I reach back into the memory of that experience, parts of it are covered in mist and images come back to me unclear and jumbled. I know we moved, we were encouraged to do so, as we raised the energy together. I know words were spoken and the rhythm surged through us. But more than that is hard to say. It isn't like remembering a dream. Rather, it feels like the sensory memories of dull yellow-brown light and the feeling of the carpet beneath my shoes and the sound of indistinct voices raised in acts of spoken magick, exultant and commanding, are all that will return to me, passing through some sort of wall.

But I remember that something changed. I believe it was a signal from the priestess guiding the ritual. It may have been an instruction for us, the participants, to change what we were doing. It may have been something within me that shifted. Exactly what it was that caused the change is unclear. What I do remember is a sense of separation from the rest of the ritual and its participants, as if everyone else flew off into space and I stayed rooted. I was a tree surrounded by birds taking flight. I found my way to the floor and sat, legs crossed and eyes closed. My awareness of the rest of the ritual going on around me is completely gone.

My experience was down on the earth. There was brown darkness behind my eyelids as I sat, my back curved over in an involuntary hunch. For a while, I tried to find and follow the guidance of the ritual but it may as well not have been there. It was that inner struggle that brought me to my second dance with the Giants.

Though no images came to me, I heard, in my mind, a deep resonant voice saying, "let them go up. You belong here with us." I knew with a deep certainty that these were the Giants. The power of the voice was similar to that I had heard when dancing in the storm two years prior. These were the vast archetypal Spirits of the Land and I could feel the weight of their voices rooting me to the earth like blankets imbued with the weight of stones, trees, and mountains.

Momentarily I worried I was missing out on some celestial adventure as the other participants journeyed amongst the stars. Briefly I worried that I hadn't done the ritual correctly or hadn't followed instructions, my "good little boy" syndrome flaring slightly, wanting to get it right. I learned then that the voice of a Giant can cut through that doubt, as surely as lightning cuts through the air. They spoke within me, telling me that, while the power of the magician to connect with the celestial is beautiful and bright, my work as a witch is rooted in the earth and the immensity of the Giants. They seemed to say "you're one of us," of course not a Giant, but a being deeply rooted in the power of this earth. An abiding sense of belonging and purpose warmed me, perhaps like the power of the sun flowing through the rest of the ritual.

When the ritual came to a close, I had no recollection of the ceremony that occurred around me while I communed with the Giants. I returned to my body at the prompting of the ritual guide, though no other instructions had made it through to me before then. It still surprises me, even after decades of learning and practice, that when I have no apparent sense or memory of a ritual, I can still be fully responsive to prompts subconsciously. The mind and magick are such fascinating things! But I digress.

When the ritual came to a close and I had no recollection of what had occurred around me, only the memory of the connection with the Giants, I came away with a new sort of calling. Perhaps it was the tension between the celestial ritual and my own earth-bound experience that made it possible to really hear and feel what seems to have been uniquely mine in that moment. It was an awareness that my work, magickal first, but also mundane and practical, is rooted in the power of Nature here on the land. The calling, this second dance with the Giants, was an invitation to dig deeper into their mythical and tangible realities, to begin to understand how to build a relationship with them.

Since then, I have explored the places in nature that I have known for a long time, with a new attention to seeing beyond what meets the eye. I have witnessed new places, seeking out new experiences with the land in order to learn and grow more. I have continued to dance in offering, both on my own and for audiences, to be able to connect with the land. I have also begun to open up to a wider understanding of what the Giants may be, as ideas and cultural movements that take on life of their own. All of this to accept the invitation and answer the call of the Giants. All of this to weave a relationship. All of this to see what comes next. And so the dance continues.

BAD NEIGHBORS

"Solving the climate crisis is the greatest and most complex challenge that homo sapiens have ever faced. The main solution, however, is so simple that even a small child can understand it."
- Greta Thunberg

"This is my home, this is my only home,
This is the only sacred ground that I have ever known,
Should I stray in the dark night alone,
Rock me Goddess in the gentle arms of Eden"
- Dave Carter and Tracy Grammer, Gentle Arms of Eden

Once upon a time, I knew a family that was surprisingly close with their neighbors. A long while ago, they actually lived in one house all together, but that was before life got in the way, the kids came, lifestyles shifted, and the family I knew decided they needed their own space. At the same time, they valued their deep friendship and they wanted to stay close to their neighbors, so they moved into a house that was so close, it nearly touched their former shared home.

For a while, not much changed. They visited each other almost every day. They cooked together and spent time just being, sharing everything like they did when they lived in the same house. By all accounts, it was a decent arrangement, if not quite the same. It served their purposes, both the family and the neighbors, because their lives really were changing and sometimes it's just better to have space of one's own as that happens.

Now, the family I knew, we'll call them the Hosaps, were really into self-improvement. They were always looking for ways to *do it better*, *make it easier*, or *be more efficient*, in almost every aspect of their lives. They said they were doing it for their children and grandchildren, that it would make them more money, make them more influential, make their lives better in general. Maybe it started that way, but over time it began to feel as if their drive towards progress was fueled solely by their desire for more, whatever "more" might mean.

The neighbors, on the other hand, were a bit more traditional, in the truest sense of the word. They were comfortable in their ways of doing things, passed down over centuries, slowly and deliberately, following the stories of the seasons. They cultivated a huge garden, growing beans, squash, and corn for food along with a wealth of other colorful and hearty plants of all kinds. They grew flowers and herbs for medicine and the sweet and spicy aromas wafted across the garden on warm summer days. The neighbors shared their bounty willingly and openly with the Hosaps, just as they had done when they lived together. The Hosaps appreciated this slower way of living in theory, but the more they progressed into their high-tech lives, the less time they took to appreciate it in reality.

Actually, the more the Hosaps progressed into their high-tech lives and passed that mentality on to their children, the more they let go of their relationship with their neighbors. They grew distant, no longer sharing the bounty that they cultivated, even though the neighbors never stopped sharing theirs with the Hosaps. The shared meals and time spent together dropped off to once a week, then to a couple of times a month, then only holidays. Finally, it dwindled until they went whole years without so much as a shared cup of coffee, which the neighbors had ground specially to share with the Hosaps, I might add. On occasion, the Hosaps might wave across the driveway as they ran in or out, hurrying here and there in their busy and important lives. They might say "hi" or "how ya doin'" in passing now and then, but overall, they lost touch with their neighbors who had once been such close friends, family even, nearly entirely.

All the while that the Hosaps had been building their new and faster, more productive, lifestyle and passing it on to their children, they had neglected some particulars of upkeep on their house. A slow drip had started at some point, who knows how long ago, from a pipe in the basement. Someone had probably spotted it but figured it wouldn't be that much of an issue. After a while though, it did get worse and the drip became a slow but steady leak. Part of the issue was likely that there were too many people living in the house without sufficiently caring for it, but when you're busy and thriving sometimes it's easy to put those things out of mind, isn't it?

A few years went by and the steady leak became steadily worse. After the Hosaps couldn't fully ignore the problem any more, I'm a bit ashamed to say that they just moved some of their belongings out of the basement and closed the door. They decided that eventually something might have to be done about the slowly-flooding basement, but overall, it would be fine, even if the water caused some damage. I think the older generation of the Hosap family might have even begun to think of the leak as something their children could deal with at some distant time down the road, but why bother with it now? Anything to not have to think about it!

Another year or two went by and the family was thriving, bigger and wealthier than ever, but their house was not. And really, under the surface, neither were they. The Hosaps were becoming cold and sharp, and frankly I didn't want to spend much time with them myself. But at least they were successful, right? To me, it all seemed like a bit much, and while people looked up to them, there wasn't much to recommend them personally any more. Most people began to see them, and treat them, as the distant, hard-hearted people they had become.

Then one day, the Hosaps heard a rumble from the basement. The shock forced them to consider that they couldn't ignore the leak any more, and let me tell you, they still tried. Finally giving in, they pried open the door that had been shut for far too long, exposing the expanding wreckage. They carefully stepped down the first few steps of the old, now-rotting wooden stairs, just to the level that wasn't submerged in murky water. They looked around and took stock of the damage. The walls were covered in slimy mildew above the still-rising waterline. There was mold growing in patches all through the support beams. The stale and damp smell of decaying, waterlogged wood was overwhelming. Many of the appliances had rusted. Really, it was a wonder there hadn't been a major fire or electrical short. Then they noticed a scorch mark on a far wall; there actually had been a small fire that must have, by some miracle, been smothered by the water enough to prevent it spreading to the whole house. That really scared the Hosaps, not realizing how close they had been to losing their home, or worse.

And finally, peering through the dank darkness at the devastation, they found the source of the rumble. Some masonry from the foundation wall of the basement closest to the neighbors' house had crumbled and splashed into the water, leaving a gaping hole from the ceiling down to the waterline where the water had started to flow slowly but steadily out. That confused the Hosaps because, by all rights, there should have been solid ground beyond that wall, at least for a few feet before the foundation of the neighbors' house began. Shining the thin beam of a flashlight towards the breach, they became horrifyingly aware that their foundation shared a wall with their neighbors' basement. They had moved into homes so close together, they were practically two parts of a whole, and now the water that had done such damage, that they had *allowed* to do such damage, was streaming into their neighbors' basement, most likely causing a massive amount of damage there too.

The Hosaps were beside themselves, but here's the funny thing, they *still* tried to ignore the problem! They turned a blind eye, hoping that whatever damage they were doing to the neighbors' house would go unnoticed or, at the very least, that the neighbors would also ignore it. It stood to reason, didn't it, that the neighbors might not want to bother talking about it, considering how long it had been since they'd had any contact between them at all? But the damage was certainly being done.

It wasn't until the Hosap children, who were just coming into their own as young adults, decided to do something about it, that anything was done at all. The children didn't have much money of their own, at least not yet, and while their parents refused to take action other than some small fixes, they struggled to figure out what to do. Realizing the situation was far bigger than they could handle on their own, the children plucked up their courage and their desperation, and without their parents' knowledge, they went and knocked on the neighbors' door.

It took a long while and several knocks for the neighbors to answer. When the door finally squealed open, the neighbors looked like they'd been asleep, maybe for a long time. They were a bit worse for wear, as if they'd been struggling to make ends meet, though the children knew their garden was still lush, at least in some places. Their handmade clothes, once well-kept and beautiful, were wrinkled and waning thread-bare. Their hair was disheveled and they looked thin and tired. And yet, they still had a strength about them that felt both impressive and imposing to the Hosap children who had come to entreat them for help.

They told the neighbors what happened, what had been happening, for such a long time. The neighbors listened with concern, but no surprise, showing on their faces as the children detailed the story of the last several years, apology and desperation clear in their voices.

"To be honest, our parents knew, and so did we, but we didn't realize, well, at least not at first, how bad it was. And we definitely didn't know, well again, not at first, that it would damage your home too. And if we're really being honest, we may have known for a little while now, and we are sorry. But now that we see how bad it is and our parents still won't do anything to stop it, we're trying to figure out what to do. We can't afford to fix it on our own. Could you help us?"

The neighbors stood staring dumbstruck for quite some time at the implications of what the Hosap children were asking. When they were finally able to speak, they confronted the children in return. "You've known about this damage for how long, and you want us to pay to fix your problem? We haven't seen you or your family for years. We used to be friends, family even, and we were more than happy to share everything with you, but now that you've caused this problem that not only affects you but has damaged our home too, you want us to fix it?" When the children didn't answer except with looks of shame and desperation, the neighbors continued. "The fact of the matter is, we don't actually need to fix this problem. We care, or more precisely, we used to care, but it is difficult to worry about people who have ignored us for such a long time, even when we used to be so close. True enough, waiting may do some damage to our home, but based on what you've told us, your family is likely to have to leave long before things get bad enough for us to need to do anything about it. When that happens and you're not here letting the leak get even worse, we'll start on the work to fix what was damaged. It may take us a while but we can wait it out."

Weighed down by the truth of what the neighbors were saying, the Hosap children apologized again and left, stricken, to try to figure out what to do. What options were left? They could pressure their parents to finally pay attention and repair the damage both to their own house and for the neighbors. They could piecemeal their own solutions to the problem, hopefully making up for lost time. They could try to make some changes to the way they lived in the house that might, at least in some small way, keep the leak from getting worse. But they also knew that they would need help from others if they were going to try to make it without their parents' assistance or acknowledgement. If the only ones who were strong enough to help were the neighbors, then the children would have to start building a bridge back to the way things used to be with them. It seemed a daunting idea, so much time had passed and so much had changed, but if they could manage to reconnect, maybe it would be better for everyone.

And that's where we are now. I'm not sure how this story ends. For myself, I hope the children pull through. I hope they're able to fix the leak, even if it's little by little. I think some bigger fixes are necessary, and fast, because at some point, damage like that reaches a tipping point and there's no going back, but that's just my opinion. And I hope they're able to rebuild a relationship with the neighbors. Honestly, knowing how close the Hosaps used to be with their neighbors, that's what I want the most out of all of this. I think it would make everything so much better for everyone involved if they were able to find a way back to each other. All that time spent together, the way they all used to thrive by learning from one another, how happy they all were; nothing is perfect and change is natural, but sometimes we lose some of the best parts of ourselves in the process if we don't pay attention. I hope the Hosaps can find those forgotten parts of themselves and be good neighbors again, and I hope I get to see it.

THE GIANTS DON'T
CARE: A COMPANION
TO BAD NEIGHBORS

We were once deeply connected with the cycles of Nature. In that connection, we shared everything, gathering our sustenance directly from the earth, knowing how to dance with the seasons to sustain ourselves without over-burdening the land on which we lived. We gave thanks for what was taken and our care for the land in return helped it to thrive.

It is a relatively recent concept that we are somehow separate from the natural world. We have shut ourselves off in boxes, treating nature as if it is nothing more than a pretty place to visit and otherwise, an inconvenience, as if we are better or more civilized than the wild forces that exist beyond the walls of our houses. When we began to separate ourselves from the natural ebb and flow of the land, we did not take into consideration, at least at first, what the separation would mean for both ourselves and our neighbors, the natural world. As we developed technology to make life easier and more profitable, we created distractions that have taken us further and further away from our neighbors and what made our relationship with them good. Those same distractions have taken us away from ourselves. Furthermore, we have allowed those distractions and the supposed ease with which modern life comes to us, to turn us away from the havoc we are wreaking on the natural world so that we can pretend it is not happening.

Even in the language describing the situation we've caused, there is an inherent assumption of the separation between us and Nature. Nature is somehow outside, out there somewhere beyond the limits of our civilized world. This is a false idea. We are part of nature. We are one and the same. We are more than neighbors sharing a foundation. Whether we accept it or not, we are still living in the same house and that house is not only leaking, it is burning.

In my search for a way to engage with the governmental powers that are allowing this damage to continue, and worse, actively perpetuating it, I went to the land, to the Giants and the spirits, and I asked for help. After all, these spirits are so much bigger than we are. I was met with a difficult but all-too-understandable response...The Giants Don't Care. And why should they? We are burning down the home we live in together, but we will disappear long before the Giants will. Then they can rebuild without us.

None of this is to say that the situation is hopeless. Far from it! I am not even telling this story to imply that technology and progress is bad. In fact, in many ways, it will help us to heal the damage we've done. It is also not meant to romanticize nature and the way things were "before." I am aware that life was difficult and dangerous and that we, as humans, built the walls we did in order to better survive. That is not a bad thing.

What I am saying, is that we have to make a concerted effort to show our neighbors that we want to return to a relationship that is truly good for us all. There is power in what we have built, the research and technology that can help and heal. But we are still under the illusion of separation from the world that we are very much a part of. We have to find our way back to living in the cycles we have come to think of as beyond or beneath us. We have to return to indigenous wisdom, to nature-based science, to spirituality, but most of all to listening to the land and hearing what it has to tell us about how to live well. Until we can do that, Nature will continue to tell us that we are no longer being good neighbors, with storms and wildfires and floods and droughts and searing heat.

The Giants are speaking as we continue to do damage, whether we are listening or not. When we can return to ourselves and some of the ways we used to live with our neighbors, we can begin to heal together.

Conclusion to A Prelude to Dancing with Giants

I t seems like a funny thing, to explain why this is a *Prelude* nearly at the end of the book, and yet, that's precisely how I want to conclude. I have spent the majority of this book introducing you to my work, laying foundations, sharing thoughts and ideas, telling stories, and generally getting to share with you the Magic that I love. And I'll bet you've got it drilled into your head now, after seeing it numerous times, how much of an *introduction* this is. So here it is, in writing...

A Prelude to Dancing with Giants, is the *prelude* to not one, but two books that I am dreaming up. The first is *Movement and Magick*, which is based on the series of workshops I have been teaching over the course of the last five years. The second, *Dancing with Giants*, is a massive (yes pun intended) project that will include a great deal of research, both academic and personal, about the Giants. The essays and stories in this book are excerpts from the work that I have begun to collect and coalesce towards bringing those pieces to life.

I cannot say when these books will become physical manifestations of the ideas dancing around in my head, but now that this *prelude* is in hand and I have made that walk down the stage on my toes, the next steps in the dance are becoming more clear. For now, I am thrilled to be able to share what I have in this introduction. I am excited to continue teaching, and certainly learning, from the process.

And while the continuing creative, and indeed magic(k)al, process that will go into these works is waltzing up a storm of excitement, there is something important that sits beyond and beneath that goal. Deep at the heart of all of this work, the writing, the teaching, the sharing, the movement and dance, the magick and spirituality, the Giants, and the Land, is the reason for all of it. I see magick and spirituality as both a means and a calling to do what we can to bring about some Good in the world. As witches, magicians, artists, healers...as people...we have a responsibility to use what we have, our gifts, to make the world a little better as we move through it. I believe that if we lean into what we are and what we have to offer, we really can do that.

My magic(k)al work is to support Nature, to heal people physically and spiritually, and to share my experience of how to do that with people who are called to learn. That is why I've gathered this book together and taken the steps to share it. I believe, in opening up, stepping forward with my stories and my joy within them, my Work will grow and I can answer the Call. I hope that, in reading *A Prelude to Dancing with Giants*, you can feel the taproots of that Work as they reach out into the world. And I hope that your Work is Calling to you too.

Thank you for reading this beginning, this *Prelude*. May you find joy in the Dance!

Section IV: Little Gifts

LITTLE GIFTS

The last movement of this *Prelude* is my way of offering you something a bit different. It is made up of just a few little gifts for you that spiral like eddies outside of the flow of the rest of the pieces in this book.

The first, *The Color of Finding Home*, is a story that I wrote about my time living in Glasgow and the visceral experience of the colors. It was previously published in *Flora Magazine's* Fall 2020 issue, *Changing Colors*. The second story, *The Stolen Child Amidst the Hemlocks*, is a surreal and wintry dream that grew from the seed of the question, "Am I a Changeling?". These stories are about senses and experiences of the fantastical magic that exists in our world.

The final piece is a poem, but also a how-to. *Breathe with the Ocean* is an invitation to do just that. I wonder what magic you may find in it.

I hope these little gifts leave you with a sense of calm, contemplation, and especially a little bit of wonder.

Enjoy!

THE COLOR OF
FINDING HOME

When I arrived, I was far too exhausted to notice the colors. They didn't register until a few days later when the weariness wore off and I was able to truly open my eyes and look around: everything was brown.

"This city is so brown," she said, and it was. The sandy brick tenements standing since the Industrial Revolution; the burnt coffee-colored water of the vast river that split the city in two; the oil-slick pavement on the relentlessly rainy days; they were all shades of brown.

The familiar land I had come from was brown too, in its own way, when I left. The last stand of the summer's conquering heat had seen to that. Over many years, I had come to expect that the tired plants would soon reanimate for one last crimson performance before sleeping through winter. However, at the end of August when I left, everything was buff, tan, scorched. Even the grass, vibrant green in spring, seemed breathless and choked. It mirrored the way I felt; listless, dry, and longing for a deep drink of the silvery forest green that awaited me across the ocean.

And then I left.

But what I saw on the other side was nothing like I'd imagined. It wasn't until late autumn that I really began to awaken to the reality of my new surroundings. I expected at least some color other than brown to emerge. I was to be disappointed. The leaves, stubbornly holding onto the dull olive color that bordered on brown for far longer than I imagined they could, weren't going to ignite like they did in the place I'd left. Come the short dusky days of early winter, the leaves simply paled and gave up as the rain battered them to the ground. It was gray heavy rain, not even the pearly blankness of white snow. Just gray that amplified the brown.

That was when I knew that I had really left, and suddenly I felt sadness over what I had lost in the transaction. Where were the trees? Not the ones in the parks. Not the ones placed there, curated to feel like a forest. Where were the real, true, wild trees whose leaves would burst into flaming glory before shedding 'til spring or shine emerald through the winter?

I was in a new world. Well, it was an old world, but I was new in it. Even when I left the city, thinking to escape into a romanticized daydream of color in the hills and valleys, they too were an optical illusion of russets and beiges that seemed to go on forever. I was a stranger in a strange land with new words, new habits, new smells, new rhythms, and one old color. And I felt swallowed in it.

Until I let go and gave in to the colors.

Slowly I began to perceive the pink of the roses along the pathway home. Those roses lasted well into the winter. Clearly it required a heartier soul than I'd seen before to glow with a bright blush like that even through the bleak, icy rain. Then I began to recognize the sky. Where the leaves refused the fiery display, the sky blossomed each night into an undeniable shock of pink, gold, and violet when the sun dropped between the steely cover of the ever-present clouds and the mahogany horizon.

At the very depth of winter, I journeyed by train far from the city, to the literal ends of the earth in this new old land. I crossed a channel of the northern ocean, the color of a hazel eye; mostly mottled steel blue shocked with a profound fir green otherwise barely present in this land. I arrived in the inky night, with not a light to pollute the sky; only the nearly-full cat eye moon.

The morning on the shortest day was gossamer golden through mist and purple hills. This landscape wasn't brown; it was vibrant with stony shades and heathered fields, and even, as I finally was able to see, deep forest-green grasses jeweled with drops in the floating silver fog and sunlight. No, there were no trees, but through the mist I had finally found my eyes and could really see the nuance of color throughout the new land. The sunset, barely five hours later, brought with it a scarlet glow that cast lavender shadows long across the fields. The full ivory moon rose brighter in the twilight verdigris than I had seen in years.

The next morning, I set out for my return to the city in the dun darkness. As I traveled, I noted newly the blues mixed with browns and whites along the way, browns that were now croissant crust golden and agate rust. February brought early cherry blossoms, rosy pale breathing life into the gray washed sepia days. Spring brought such vibrant flowers of crimson and coral that I was compelled to sit and breathe in the smoldering glow, even when they were in the curated forests. The hills were now tawny brush shot through with gorse orange and heather purple that met the watery blue-gray sky.

The cycle began again but I finally understood it. As I let myself see the colors, they changed in front of my eyes and I let this new old world, so different from what I'd imagined and so different from the place I had known before, become a home.

THE STOLEN CHILD
AMIDST THE
HEMLOCKS

"Come away oh human child,
to the waters and the wild,
with a fairy hand in hand,
for the world's more full of weeping than you can understand."
W.B. Yeats, *The Stolen Child*

On the southern side of the mountain, along Jack Frost Trail, over the crest of the hill and down through the natural gateway of pines towards the west, there is a vast grove of hemlock trees. Hemlocks, long-lived and sturdy through the winter, are full of memory. In this grove on the shielded side of the mountain, the trees stretch tall to the sky and create a sanctuary of columns where memories echo in the stillness. The perfect moment to hear these echoes is the first snowfall of winter, when the only sound is the fingertip-soft patter of the feathery flakes on the recently fallen leaves.

Many times, I've made my way up the mountainside in the

silvery light of the first snowfall, each year savoring the quiet solitude of the grove, protected by the hemlock sentinels as the frozen drops fall. On one such afternoon of a recent year, I encountered a memory I did not expect, or maybe it was a dream.

The first flakes had come and I rushed to the mountain, slinking away from my responsibilities as stealthily as I could. My usual hiking gear of gray work boots and matching coat, faded blue jeans, my father's old machine-knitted sweater, and the cobalt blue wrap I'd worn as a scarf every winter for years, held in my warmth as I embarked on my traditional journey. I left my car, the only vehicle in the lot, and rushed my way across the road to the trailhead. With the fervent flood of excitement and the fresh energy that rules the first steps of a hike, I bounded up the initial climb of the trail and into the forest. The steely air shocked my nose and lungs but the slight sweetness frozen into it promised a perfect first snow, making every shiver worthwhile.

As I climbed, my steps became heavier, my legs aching with the exertion and cold. Some might say that I was too young to feel so worn out so quickly, but I was certainly not a child anymore and my knees were all too ready to tell me so. Nonetheless, I made my way along the trail, scaling the rocky paths, catching sinewy young tree trunks for support, and finally reaching the forested plateau that led the last little way towards my hemlock cathedral. Dark emerald shadows mixed with pale sepia where the trail eased to a much gentler incline, winding through a thicket of winter-withered ferns, shielded from the winds from the southwest by a barrier of pine boughs.

Finally reaching the branched gateway through the gnarled and wind-bent pines, I ascended the last weathered-stone hill and looked down into the sheltered glen surrounded by hemlocks. On this particular day, as I climbed down towards the grove, I found, thoroughly out of place in the middle of the winding path, a tall oval dressing room mirror, set in a wooden frame on hinges that let it swing forward and back. The glass flashed my reflection back at me as I approached this absurd intrusion in the forest. My nerves fluttered at the unsettling sight, but my hesitation began to mix with a peculiar sense of familiarity and even, in some strange way, a feeling of invitation and welcoming. I found the mirror to be just my height, reflecting my entire form against the backdrop of the woods around me. Perplexed, I wondered who would be eccentric enough to carry such an odd piece of furniture up the mountainside.

Examining myself in the mirror, I felt a strange suspicion that the reflection of me was, in some way, more than a mere image. As I took in my appearance, I developed the distinct sense that my mirrored self was somehow also a living me, only standing on the other side. I looked down at the brown leather cuff that I wore on my right wrist. Suddenly, but also as if it had never been otherwise, the cuff was on my left wrist. I looked up to find myself on the other side of the glass, facing back the way I'd come, though no reflection remained.

Perhaps I should have been more startled but before there was a chance for any shock to settle in, the silence of the first snow was broken by a bright reverberation of joyous laughter behind me in the grove. The mirror forgotten, I whirled around and saw, a little way off between the trees, a young boy. No more than four or five years old, he was swaddled in a puffy red nylon coat, royal blue sweat pants, and little black and white patterned sneakers. He was running and jumping off of stones, catching snowflakes with an abandon I had not seen, and certainly not felt, in ages. Something about the playfulness that radiated from the small child jarred my heart with the most wrenching mix of sadness and yearning, nostalgia, and bittersweet happiness. I was stunned into stillness by the exquisite ache, remembering a time when, like the boy, my only responsibility had been to play. In the stark contrast of his laughter to my own staid restraint, I wondered when I had lost that part of myself. When did that child in me disappear?

Shaking myself out of my pensive stupor, it suddenly occurred to me to wonder where the boy's parents might be. There was no obvious sign of anyone else in the woods. Growing a bit concerned, I made my way down amongst the trees where the boy was playing. I rounded a particularly large trunk and found that he was not, if fact, alone at all. Beyond the first few hemlock trunks stood a woman and a man. The woman, whose appearance was the truest definition of the word ethereal, was clad in a long white dress that danced gently in the frozen air. Her hair and skin were so pale, they nearly matched the falling snow. The man had a feral quality, not unkind but certainly more earthy, as if he might, at any point, sniff the breeze and run off into the trees. He wore trousers that gave the impression of fur and a rough linen shirt that matched his skin perfectly. Both had the appearance of youth but seemed, at the same time, undeniably mature, even timeless. For some reason, neither seemed to notice the cold chill, no sign of a shiver running through either of them. Stranger still, in flashes so brief I felt as though I'd imagined them, the woman gave off the distinct impression that she was glowing, like full moonlight on snow, and the man appeared to have antlers.

I might have assumed that these two beings, for any other word seems inadequately precise to describe them, were the parents of the little boy. I might have, that is, except that he was everything they were not. Both the woman and the man were unmistakably, and paradoxically, poised yet wild, serene yet alert, withheld yet present, and completely otherworldly, wholly unreal. I recognized a bit of their countenance in myself, if I'm honest, a version of their composure and distance mirrored in me. The little boy was so very different, unapologetically alive, loud, and boisterous, without fear or restraint, as he reveled in the snowy pre-dusk evening. More than anything, he was real in a way that the woman and man absolutely were not.

I edged closer to the three of them, trying unsuccessfully to stifle my footsteps in the crisp dryness of the early winter. When even my quiet footfalls interrupted the sounds of his play, the boy spun and froze mid-run. He paused, clearly unsure what to make of me, then turned and, as any shy child will do when meeting a grownup, ran to the possibly-antlered man for comfortable familiarity, who lofted him up in his arms. Assessing me with an air of knowing something I did not, the silver woman and the wild man watched me for a moment. Silently, the three moved towards me. The man stepped deer-like, with the boy in his arms, deliberately placing foot after foot on the soft beds of decaying hemlock needles. The woman was a whisp of wind, her bare feet seeming to miss the ground entirely with each step, though they stirred the dry fallen leaves as she moved. They stopped a short distance away. The man held the boy close and, regarding me with a smile in his eye, said something quietly to the boy that made him turn his head and gape at me with wide eyes.

Setting the boy back down, the man and woman took his hands and came a bit closer. As they drew near, a shock set in. With an excited, inquisitive smile, the boy looked up at me. Staring at me were my own stormy blue eyes. It was then I realized that I knew the little boy and he knew me.

"I want to grow up to be just like you someday!" he exclaimed exuberantly.

I laughed deeply and brightly for the first time in what must have been years. "I want to grow up to be just like you!" I said right back.

As if she'd always been there, my own mother was

standing between the antlered man and the shining woman, dressed warmly in her black suede coat lined with faux fur. Beside her was my father in his padded parka and worn-out loafers, not quite right for the cold. They moved towards me, the smaller version that is, and picked me up between them. Looking back at me, little me said excitedly, "Mommy, Daddy look, that's me." They smiled at me silently with knowing pride at seeing the man their little boy would become. But they also looked from me to little me and back, a quiet but clear reminder that the childlike wonder never had to leave me, that it was still in me somewhere, waiting. They hugged little me closer between them and, putting him down again, took his hands and went off to play in the snow before the dark set in.

I stood silently in the gloaming amidst the hemlocks and the falling snow, the antlered man on my left and the shining woman on my right, watching the little boy and his parents play. Standing there with the two beings, I was overtaken with an otherworldly stillness, but it was a stillness I recognized in myself, one I'd felt often. For better or worse, the quiet resolve that held me still and silent was a near-constant companion on the normal side of the mirror, back in the real world. It kept me safe, only showing the reflection of what I wanted people to see. It was powerful, but also restrictive.

Here, amidst the hemlocks, seeing the self, the little boy, that this preternatural composure had supplanted, I felt a longing to let it all go and dance, swirling through the flakes over the ground as drifts of white collected in corners of stone and at the bases of the soaring columns of the trees. I felt the desire welling in me to simply allow all of that joy within me to flow free and unfettered. Yet with all of that dancing inside of me, I kept still, standing there with my silent companions. I don't know how long I was there with them in whatever mirror world or fairy land I might have entered, but for a while it was a simple joy to watch and listen as the snow fell and the child I used to be, played again for the first time in years.

After some time, I realized that I was alone again, the fae woman and man gone, and the little boy, me, and his, my own, parents faded into memory or dream. But the woods were anything but silent. There was joyous laughter, deep and hearty. There was the heavy thumping of boots on frozen ground and the swish of winter fabric as sleeves slid over the torso of a coat. As if it had never been otherwise, I found myself running and jumping from rocks, catching the snow that was blowing from the needled hemlock branches, forked like antlers. The full moon rising over the eastern path down into the hemlock grove, just beyond sunset, was shining on the newly-laid snow, my swirling boot prints catching the soft beams of light. The mirror was gone and my leather cuff was back on my right wrist where it began. I was where I began too. And I was playing.

Breathe with the Ocean

Inhale as the sea pulls back from the shore
Fill your lungs with the potential of the tides, And wait
in the swell just a little bit more
Until...

Exhale as the waves crest and crash
The relief and release of letting go, And reach
with fingers of foam that spray and splash
Until...

Inhale the tumbling of pebbles turning to sand
Singing their susurration in the wave's retreat, And curl
a current of coaxing that laps at the land
Until...

Exhale with the push and the power
Of immeasurable expanses drifting and driving, And fill
each cove and crevice to surge up and shower
Until...

Inhale the ease of surrender to the moon
Lay back and dissolve to dance on the edge of the inevitable,
And rise
to her pull, then drop to the swoon
Until...

Exhale as the sea joins the land
A moment of calm balance, between and fleeting, And settle
quiet, to begin the cycle again as Nature has planned
Until...

ABOUT THE AUTHOR

Christopher Croucher, Stormdancer, is an artist, performer, healer, and witch, who lives for the magic of the world; those beautiful, subtle, glorious moments that are beyond the sum of their parts and fill us with a sense of wonder. His work and his art, which in many ways are one and the same, take the form of dance and performance art, painting, fiber arts, writing, music, and anything that takes his fancy in a given moment. His work as a massage therapist and Magickal Healer gives him the opportunity to interact closely with people, while his environmental dance work, Letting the Land Lead, allows him to stay connected to the earth. All of it weaves together and is deeply rooted in his nature-based spiritual practice which serves as a throughline in all aspects of his life.

Magic has been a part of Chris's life since he was a very young child, as has his love of dance, both beginning to take root in his life before the age of three. He cultivated his practices of magic(k) and art through his young life and teenage years, then through his time at Bard College studying dance composition, the Cortiva Institute, where he became massage therapist, and at the Glasgow School of Art, where he received his Master of Letters in Fine Art Practice - Performance in 2019.

Now back home in central Massachusetts, Chris, or Storm as he is becoming known in his spiritual communities, shares his love of magic(k) by teaching, performing, choreographing, and doing healing work with clients and classes. His business, Doorway In Arts, serves as an umbrella for all the many facets of his work. At the core of it all, Chris is driven by the joy of reveling in magic and sharing it with those who feel called to its pull.

Image List

Front Cover
Giant of the Storm
Christopher Croucher
Watercolor and Acrylic on Paper
November 2025

Where the Three Realms Meet
Christopher Croucher
Acrylic and Silicone on Canvas
March 2024

Still from *Letting the Land Lead: Summer in the Fields*
Filmed by Brian Cowe
Choreography Christopher Croucher
Summer 2023

Forest Dance
Lindsay Hite Photography
September 2021

Autumn Oak Leaf
Christopher Croucher
Watercolor and Acrylic on Paper
August 2024

Marginal Way
Christopher Croucher
Watercolor and Handmade Ink on Paper
2022

Back Cover
The Sleeping Giant
Christopher Croucher
Watercolor and Acrylic on Paper
November 2025

Author's Photo
Lindsay Hite Photography